Copyright © 2018 Melvin Orange

The right of Melvin Orange to be identified as the Author of the Work has been asserted by him in accordance with the Copyright.

All rights reserved. No part of this book may be reproduced, stored in a retrieval system, or transmitted in any form by any means, electronic, mechanical, photocopying, recording, or otherwise without prior written permission of the publisher, nor be otherwise circulated in any form of binding or cover other than that in which it is published and without a similar condition being imposed on the subsequent purchaser, except in the case of brief quotations embodied in critical articles and reviews.

First Edition

Published in 2018 by Melvin Orange

Printed in the United States of America

327

THE

AFRICAN

PHILOSOPHY

BY:

MELVIN ORANGE JR.

CONTENTS

INTRODUCTION 1

THE FATHER 9

THE BEGINNINGS 27

MOUNT OLYMPUS 47

THE SPIRITUAL WORLD 63

THE ROMAN EMPIRE 83

THE RENAISSANCE 95

MARTIN LUTHER 109

ABRAHAM LINCOLN 135

THE GREAT DEPRESSION............ 151

MARTIN LUTHER KING JR. 165

MODERN DAY SLAVERY 185

THE UNIVERSAL SPIRIT 203

THE REVOLUTION 227

THE UNIVERSAL SPIRITUAL FATHER................. 253

SUPERSTAR 269

THE AUTHORS LAST WORDS................. 270

"I Will Send My Spirit In All Men And Women, Then Your Sons And Daughters And Future Generations Will Speak The Fathers Word. I Will Show Powerful Works In The Heavens, And On The Earth".

-MELVIN ORANGE JR.

INTRODUCTION

The most important thing in the ancient world was wisdom. The Greeks understood that wisdom was extremely important and came to believe that the wisest man, is the best man. Wisdom can be taught to anyone, because of this the Greeks invented a different form of wisdom, intelligence. Although the Greeks created intelligence, they continued their quest for wisdom, the word philosophy comes from the Greek, meaning love wisdom. Philosophy is an elevated level of thinking to establish what is known, true, and real, it also explains human action, given the limits of human thought and senses. Philosophy focuses on what human beings really know and is the only way to reflect the entirety of things. Philosophy sheds light on your place in the

Universe, it offers fresh new ways of thinking, acting, being, and seeing the world, it guides your actions and increases the quality of your life. Philosophy is what life genuinely, honestly, deeply, and absolutely means, you can't operate right without one, it shapes everything you do. It is necessary to have a philosophy, it is a personal rule of life. Everyone has a philosophy, most adopt others without knowing, it is impossible to understand the world in terms of mind looking at matter, your consciousness is most important, it is as important an element in the working of the universe, as is matter itself. To know what you are looking at in the world, you must be aware of the lens through which you view it, which is your philosophy.

With the same philosophy everyone has the same thought pattern, which eliminates division, confusion, and argument. Once you change your philosophy, you change your thought pattern; once you change your thought pattern, you change your attitude; once you change your attitude, you change your behavior pattern; and once you change your behavior pattern, you are a renewed human being that produces good action.

Learning anything new involves change, once you learned the alphabet it did not leave you, it became part of a new you, who changed through the process of learning. Philosophy has the power to send beams of light around the world, allowing human beings to see things anew.

Whenever a building is constructed you have an architect who draws a blueprint. The blueprint serves as the guide, pattern, and model for those who are to build the building. A building is not erected correctly without a good, accurate, and solid blueprint. You are in the process of building the structure of your life, and this philosophy is the blueprint. This philosophy is the universal truth, no one can deny the truth. This philosophy is designed to teach, elevate, and uplift human beings and bring everyone together, for we are all one link in a chain of being, that stretches from the past into the future.

Enter the Spiritual Realm...

THE FATHER

Before there was time and space there was the Universe. The Universe was dark, empty, and formless. Then mysteriously, the Universe creates a big bang. The big bang explosion brings into existence the first elements, they are hydrogen and helium. The element hydrogen is the number one element in life on earth and is the most common atom in the Universe and in your body. What is an atom? An atom is the essential part of the physical Universe, it is found in solids, liquids and gases. After the big bang explosion there was a time of darkness, the name of this time is the dark ages, during the dark ages elements develop into other elements and bring into existence the stars. Stars are mostly made up of hydrogen and helium. What is a star? A star is a ball of burning gas, held up by its inner pressure and held together by its own gravity. Stars are super-hot and give off a lot of light and heat. There are around 1,000,000,000,000,000,000,000 stars in the Universe now, and stars are assorted colors, like red, yellow, and blue. The sun is also a star. The suns core is around 17,000,000 degrees kelvin, creating nuclear fusion and releasing energy. The sun is an energy fireball. Stars develop and multiply over time, along with elements and then bring into existence galaxies and planets. A galaxy is a large group of stars. There are around 300,000,000,000 stars in the Milky Way galaxy now, and there are over 127,000,000,000 other galaxies that human beings know of, each one of them containing billions of stars, and in the center of each galaxy is a black hole. Black holes concentrate energy and direct the movement of the stars. Black holes move Stars around from its gravitational forces, and black holes warp time and space. Planets move around a star. The planets moving around the sun star, starting from the nearest to the sun and moving outward are Mercury, Venus, Earth,

Mars, Jupiter, Saturn, Uranus and Neptune. There are also dwarf planets such as Pluto and exoplanets such as Gliese 581g. In the search for life on different planets, human beings search for water, and there are billions of planets in the Universe, some have water beneath the surface. Greek and Roman mythology named the planets moving around the sun and gave them meaning. Earth is the only planet moving around the sun whose English name does not come from Greek and Roman mythology, the name comes from Old English and Germanic.

Mercury-The messenger god.

Mercury is the closest planet to the sun, the day side is extremely hot, and the night side is extremely cold.

Venus-The love and beauty god.

Venus is hot, the air is toxic, and it spends in the opposite direction than earth.

Mars- The war god.

Mars is a desert like, with Iron oxide dust, that gives the planet a red glow. There is a liquid body of water beneath the surface.

Jupiter- The king of the gods.

Jupiter is the largest planet, it is gassy, made up of mostly hydrogen and helium, with around

17 moons. Europa is one of the moons of Jupiter, there is a liquid body of water beneath the surface.

Saturn- The agriculture god. Saturn has three rings around it made of rock and ice. It is gassy, made up of hydrogen and helium, with over 7 moons.

Uranus- The representation of heaven.

Uranus spins on its right side, it has methane in the air that gives it a bright blue glow, and it has around 27 moons.

Neptune-The water god.

Neptune is cold and windy, it is about 17 times the size of the earth, and about 30 times as far away from the sun, then earth is.

Pluto-The underworld god.

Pluto is small, cold and rocky, and it has about 3 moons.

Earth is around 71 percent, water, and Earth has around 21 percent, oxygen with around 77 percent, nitrogen in the air. Earth's core is made of the element iron, and at the center of the Earth's core, temperatures are around 7400 degrees kelvin, hotter than the surface of the sun. Earth moves around the sun 17 miles per second, with the sun providing it with light, heat, and energy. Earth also has one of the largest moons in the solar system. You need the sun and water for basic human life, but you don't need the moon. Earth is our home, it is the 5th largest planet in the solar system moving around the sun, smaller than the gas planets, but larger than the rocky planets.

The Universe is around 13.7 billion years old, since the big bang explosion. The Universe brought earth into existence over 4.3 billion years ago, and elements formed cells underwater over 3.4 billion years ago. All human beings have one or more cells, a cell is the essential part of life. Over 537,000,000 years ago, the Universe created a Cambrian Explosion, underwater, this explosion brought human beings and animals into existence. Human beings are like animals, human beings have hair and produce milk for developing the young, like some animals, but what separates human beings from animals, is the human being's ability to act with the power of the mind. Over 417,000,000 years ago, plant life dominated the land, then around 370,000,000 years ago, the first human beings wandered to land, in Africa. Human beings have discovered a 3.2-million-year-old females bones in Africa. She was nicknamed Lucy, she was about 3 feet tall, with a head the size of a mango and a brain the size of a golf ball. Over 230,000,000 years ago, dinosaurs walk the earth and all the earths different continents were all together forming one single land, named Pangaea. Then an asteroid hit earth and wiped out almost all of life on earth and created the separation of the land, Pangaea. Over 1,000,000 years ago, the land begins to separate, and this brings into existence diverse cultures and distinct kinds of human beings and animals, changing the evolution of life. Human beings and animals could only have contact with the other human beings and animals in their land continent, in the beginning, and over time continents developed civilizations, then different civilizations began to arise. All the life on earth comes from the same elements that made the sun, the stars, the moon and all the planets in the Universe. All life on earth has DNA in common, we are all connected, everything in nature lives in the Universe, and the Universe lives within everything in nature. Everyone is related to

each other, we are all brothers and sisters, and

the Universe is the Father.

THE BEGINNINGS

In the beginnings, the African civilization was great. The African continent formed great kingdoms that developed into great empires. In the roots of the African civilization, there was the great ancient African Axumite civilization. The original ancient African civilization worshipped the Sun God Shamash, and the Moon God Almouqah.

The original Africans believed that God controlled the sun, the moon, and all the elements of nature. This is Africa's first, natural and original belief and religion. Africa and Southern Arabia worshipped the Sun God Shamash, and the Moon God Almouqah, for over a thousand years, before Christianity. The Africans mainly worshipped the Sun God Shamash, and the

Arabians mainly worshipped the Moon God Almouqah, they both had the same beliefs. The great ancient African civilization built tall tower obelisk, temples and pyramids to worship and honor the Sun God Shamash, and the Moon God Almouqah. Some of these buildings are still standing today, like the Almouqah Temple, the great Temple of the Moon, its dedicated to the Moon God

Almouqah, it is now known as the great Temple of Yeha, built in the 7th century. Underneath these tall tower obelisk and pyramids were underground tunnels that led to the tombs and treasures of African Kings. Africans were great throughout the stone age, the bronze age, and the iron age, when metal replaced bronze, Africans had knowledge of iron and of iron objects. The ancient Africans discovered, and had knowledge of all the basic ancient elements like iron, led, copper, silver, and gold. The original Africans had absolute knowledge and wisdom and thrived. In the beginnings, Africans were great, wealthy and powerful from there natural resources, religious beliefs, and position at the Horn of Africa. Ancient Africans controlled the trade routes of the

Red Sea and created African ports. The great ancient Africans did business international, and traded gold, silver, copper, bronze, emeralds, olive oil, wine, turtle shell, frankincense, and much more. Frankincense is an aromatic gum resin from African trees, used in religious ceremonial practices. Frankincense was as valuable as gold, because the smoke brought religious magical powers. Africans sold frankincense all around the world. The ancient Africans were so rich, wealthy, and powerful they had their own gold coins of currency, with their faces engraved on them. During this Golden Age, the great ancient African civilization did business and traded with other Africans, India, Persia, China, Rome, and Greece, for over 17 years.

In the 4th century, after the death of Christ, Christianity began to arise. Christianity did not exist until around 100 years after the death of Christ. After the death of Christ, Christ followers settled in Northern Africa. Christianity spread fast in Africa, and some of its Holy Scriptures were created in Africa. The essential teachings of Christianity were created and kept alive by

Africans, Africans are the authentic original Christians. In the beginning of Christianity, there were just Holy Scriptures. The original Christians had the qualities of goodness, equality, justice, righteousness, peace, respect, honesty, strength, helpfulness, truth and self-enlightenment. The ancient Africans did business often with Rome and Arabia, so Christianity spread out fast throughout the

Roman Empire and the Middle East. Constantine I of Rome, and Tiridates of Armenia, changed their religion to Christianity early. The first ancient African King to change his religion to Christianity was King Ezana, in the 4th century. Christianity spread out fast throughout different kingdoms, and each culture formed their own Christian culture. In the beginning,

Christianity brought peace and harmony between different empires. Africa and Europe were less than 17 miles apart, and Christianity brought them together. During this time soldiers, scholars, and political advisors traveled back and forth from Africa to Europe, doing business and trading. Then Islam came into being, by the Arabians. Muhammad brought Islam into being and is the essence for the Quran. Muhammad said, "While I was in a trance-like mind state, an angel appeared to me, the angel said, speak the truth in the name of the Lord who created all, speak the truth and spread out the word that the Lord is the most generous, who teaches by the pen, the Lord who teaches man what he knew not". Muhammad's teachings threatened the way of life during his time, the people in power disliked him. The first immigration of Muslims traveled to Africa. Muhammad and his followers marched to Mecca and defeated the people in power, before his death. After the death of the Prophet Muhammad, Islamic Muslim armies marched west out of Arabia, into north Africa. Islamic Muslim armies conquered parts of Africa, parts of Europe, and parts of

Spain, and with conquering these areas came a way of life. No one was forced to become a Muslim, it just happened on its own, some people changed their religion from Christian to Muslim. The Islamic Muslim religion stretched from north Africa through parts of Spain and had the power for hundreds of years. This was the Golden Age for Islam during this time, Islam advanced mathematics, medicine, and science. The Islamic Muslims created algebra, the numeral system, star maps, and much more. The star maps were created to help direct the people as a way of navigation. The Muslims also named most of the stars, that do have names for them. Muslims were great, but invasions brought down the Islamic Muslim dynasty.

In the 11th century a new African dynasty raised from the dirt, and brought back Christianity, the great African Zagwe dynasty. Out of all the Kings that would rule in the great African Zagwe dynasty, the one who stands out from the rest is King Lalibela. King Lalibela is known for creating 12 excellent, hand carved, humongous churches, each made from a single block of living rock.

These mysterious, humongous rock buildings are magnificent building constructions, they are some of the best constructions the world has to offer. Africans went from building temples, to building tall tower obelisk, to building pyramids, to building churches, and they all were majestic. King Lalibela had a vision, he said, *"God said, build a new kingdom, God said, if you build these churches that I show you, I will make you king"*, and then King Lalibela made a spiritual agreement with God. King Lalibela also said, *"The angels delivered the plans to me and guarded me day and night, as I worked on the churches for about 25 years"*. King Lalibela was made a Saint, and during his rule everything was peaceful, in unity, and righteous, he was not feared.

Religions spread fast like bestsellers.

Christianity and Islam are forced and normalized in your mind. Christianity and Islam are just different ideas and beliefs, but everyone has the same Father. The universal Spiritual Father God, the Universe, is not Christian or Islam, these are human systems created to help us walk into the mystery of the universal Spiritual Father God, the

Universe. There is only one Universal Father, the one who brought all of life into existence, the same one Universal Father who created the sun, the stars, the moon, and all the planets, the universal Spiritual Father God, the Universe.

MOUNT OLYMPUS

Before the Olympians became the gods and goddesses, there were the Titans. The Titans were the gods and goddesses of the earth, the direct descendants of heaven and earth. The Titans were a mighty, immortal, and powerful culture, race, or color. The Titans were the opposite culture, race, or color, then the Olympians, and were their arch enemy. The Titans were giant gods of wisdom, knowledge, and strength. The Titans were the gods of old beliefs, old religion rituals, and of black magic. The Titans were the first, the real, the natural, and the original gods of the earth. The Titans lived in gold palaces, with marble floors, on the highest mountain in the world. This divine, heavenly, and magnificent mountain was called Mount

Othrys, and the Titans ruled the world from the top of this mountain. When the Titans ruled, the world was in peace and harmony. The Titans controlled the sun, the stars, the moon, the planets and all the earths elements. The Titans were the descendants of Gaea and Uranus, they gave birth to 12 Titans, six were male gods, and six were female goddesses. The six male gods were Coeus,

Cronus, Crius, Hyperion, Iapetus, and Oceanus. The six female goddesses were Mnemosyne, Phoebe, Rhea, Theia, Themis, and Tethys. Each one of the gods and goddesses had their part to play in controlling the world.

Coeus- The Titan God of knowledge, intellect, and understanding.

Cronus- The Titan God of war.

Crius- The Titan God of the sky.

Hyperion- The Titan God of the sun.

Iapetus- The Titan God of life and death.

Oceanus- The Titan God of connecting the realms of God, the dead, and the living.

Mnemosyne- The Titan Goddess of wisdom.

Phoebe- The Titan Goddess of the moon.

Rhea- The Titan Goddess of motherhood.

Theia- The Titan Goddess of love, desire, and beauty.

Themis- The Titan Goddess of law and order.

Tethys- The Titan Goddess of water.

Once every red moon, the Titan gods and goddesses would gather at the highest point of Mount Othrys, and discuss the matters of the earth, to establish how they could improve it. The gods and goddesses controlled all, the heavens, the earth, and the people. The gods and goddesses controlled the people through their spiritual beliefs, and the Titan gods and goddesses were known as the elder gods. Less than 100 miles away, there were the Olympians. The Olympians were the opposite culture, race, or color, of the Titans. The Olympians were jealous, and envied the

Titans, they wanted to rule the world in their place. The Olympians teamed up with allies and grew strong, then invaded the Titans on Mount Othrys. The Olympians even released men from jail to help them in the war against the Titans, the war was named Titanomachy, the legendary Battle of the Titans. The war would last over 7 years, with the Olympians coming out on top. The

Olympians overthrew the Titans, in the Battle of the Titans, and took over their divine, heavenly kingdom. The Olympians seized Mount Othrys, and stole all the knowledge, wisdom, and treasures, from the Titans, then renamed the mountain, Mount Olympus. Then the Olympians created their own gods and goddesses, to replace the Titan gods and goddesses. The replacement of the six male gods were Zeus, Poseidon, Apollo, Ares, Hermes, and Hephaestus.

The replacement of the six female goddesses were Hera, Hestia, Artemis, Aphrodite, Demeter, and Athena.

Zeus-Became the Olympian God of the sky.

Poseidon-Became the Olympian God of water.

Apollo-Became the Olympian God of the sun.

Ares-Became the Olympian God of war.

Hermes-Became the Olympian God of intellect and business.

Hephaestus-Became the Olympian God of fire.

Hera-Became the Olympian Goddess of marriage.

Hestia-Became the Olympian Goddess of motherhood.

Artemis-Became the Olympian Goddess of the moon.

Aphrodite-Became the Olympian Goddess of love, desire, and beauty.

Demeter-Became the Olympian Goddess of agriculture.

Athena-Became the Olympian Goddess of wisdom.

Greek art shows images of the Olympian gods and goddesses, who were unjust, they would lie, steal, cheat, deceive, murder, and commit adultery. The people began worshipping demons and false gods and goddesses, and were led astray, for example, there was Oedipus, *he was deserted at birth, then was inspired by the Olympian gods and goddesses to kill his father and marry his mother.* The Olympian gods and goddesses were the opposite of the Titan gods and goddesses.

The allies of the Greeks, The Romans, named the planets after the Olympian gods and goddesses.

The Romans: Zeus = Jupiter

The Romans: Poseidon = Neptune

The Romans: Hermes = Mercury

The Romans: Ares = Mars

The Romans: Aphrodite = Venus

The Romans: Hades = Pluto

After defeating the Titans, the Olympians took over the divine, heavenly, and magnificent mountain of the Titans, Mount Othrys, and renamed it Mount Olympus. After stealing the knowledge, wisdom, and treasures of the Titans, the Olympians dominated the people, the heavens and the earth. The Olympians closed the golden gates that led to the highest mountain in the world, and guarded them, so no one could get in, and because of this the Olympians maintained domination over the world and watched over human beings from the heights of Mount Olympus.

THE SPIRITUAL WORLD

The world is only a picture, projected from your brain. The key to understanding reality, is to understand the spiritual world. The appearances of things are just descriptions, for example, gold is not defined by your descriptions of it, like soft, yellow, shiny, heavy metal, but is defined by its essential property, the atomic element

79. Everything you see in the physical world has an inner spiritual world, and the truth lives within the world of appearances. Human beings are taught to focus on the appearances of things, but the eternal forms of the world, that are timeless, space less, and perfect, are in the spiritual world,

like righteousness, truth, justice, honesty, understanding, peace, goodness, happiness, and beauty. The spiritual world is an inner world, a world of things within themselves, and an eternal realm. The sense of self is not located in any part of the brain or nervous system. The spiritual world is the absolute truth of reality, and the great ancient African pyramids symbolize this search for the truth.

Everything derives from the spiritual world. Inner self-knowledge is spiritual knowledge, which is universal, changeless, and timeless. The universal spirit that is within everyone is righteous and good. The Universe is the Father of the universal spirit of goodness and righteousness, and is the author of all things beautiful, just, and right. The universe controls everything, listen to your Father, listen to the universal spirit that is within you, your conscience. Consciousness is the essence of a human being, your consciousness is your inner mind where you think, feel, plan, wish, imagine, pray, and relive experiences, it is your private thoughts and feelings.

Whatever you feed your spiritual world is what you grow into. Human beings are a bundle of thoughts, feelings, and impressions, which give you a sense of being an I. Knowledge, wisdom, and truth, goes to those who work hard for it. Have the knowledge of what is good and right and the qualities of such as justice, equality, peace, respect, helpfulness, harmony, and truth. Have the knowledge of righteous and good spiritual forms such as composure, control, temperance, self-discipline, positiveness, understanding, and equality, for these qualities to manifest themselves into actual circumstances, for it is action that forms your character. The process of finding things good or bad is the work of your imagination, perceive the unseen. To gain knowledge of the world to understand reality, information must first go through one or more of your physical sense organs, like your eyes, ears, mouth, nose, or skin, then electrical signals are sent to the brain. The understanding of reality and knowledge is connected to the way you perceive, you can only understand things as you perceive them. Something is perceived to be real, only if your lens allows it to be seen. Things exist in the context of the observer's perception of them, no two set of human beings have the exact same set of sense receptors, you see, perceive, and experience reality from your own unique way, but what we all have in common is the universal moral law, which is the sense of what is right, good, changeless, timeless, and perfect. The Universe is the Father of what you perceive, you can perceive things as they are with the right amount of knowledge and wisdom. The brain is involved in every aspect of your life, it is a complex, 3-pound structure, controlling every behavior and thought. When you think electrical and chemical signals are moving throughout your brain, creating different sensations, perceptions, and emotions, within. The front of the brain controls the most complicated functions, such as thinking and planning. The right side of the brain controls nonverbal information, such as perception and emotion. The left side of the brain controls language, speech, and grammar. At birth, a baby's brain contains around 100,000,000,000 neurons, about as many nerve cells, as there are stars in the milky way.

Human beings understand reality within 3 ways, what you think, your life experiences, and your physical sense organs. Understanding reality through the physical sense organs create physical sensations and pleasures. Physical sensations and pleasures are what human beings are attracted to the most, it is more attractive, easier, simpler, and more intense, than the pleasures of higher wisdom, higher knowledge, and higher intellect. These physical sensations and pleasures become addictive, and are instant and don't last long, for example, eating lavish gives you instant pleasure, but it will fade away and lead to dissatisfaction later. Higher wisdom, higher knowledge, and higher intellect should be your desire and it provides pleasure naturally, this kind of sensation and pleasure is absolute and eternal. Be in control of your pleasures, if an action gives you instant pleasure, but will create pain in the future, don't do it.

The world is constantly in motion, always changing, and human beings are constantly moving through experiences of, and perceptions of, it is a never-ending process of living and dying, but doing what is right and good is changeless, timeless, perfect, and universal. What is perfect does not need to change, because it is perfect. Rulers and governments, make laws for their own advantage, these laws control and manipulate situations, so that it works out in their favor. These laws are not the natural laws of the universe, but are laws for men like these, for a reason of advantage. Rulers and governments, make sure their own concerns are cared for, but don't care about the impact that it has on others. Slavery was considered all right not long ago, power structures only pay lip-service to equality, freedom, and human rights. Equality is for everyone in the world, truth, justice, righteousness, and goodness are universal forms that everyone must fight for. True freedom is spiritual. The western civilization has taught the world a left-brain way of seeing things. People are worshipping false gods and have learned to glorify the bad. Now people deceive, lie, steal, cheat, have lack of self-control, and encourage violence, these evil qualities weaken, pollute, and corrupt minds, which will eventually lead to the destruction of the world. Worshipping false gods have made being righteous and good look weak but being righteous and good, is the purpose of a human being, it is all-powerful. Human existence must turn in the right direction, which is good, just, righteous, understanding, sincere, equal, and peaceful, this is the universal way. *Doing what is right and good is the only way to secure peace on earth.* There are 2 types of people on earth, there are people who build mountains out of what is right and good and the qualities of, and there are people who destroy mountains out of

what is right and good and the qualities of.

THE ROMAN EMPIRE

The romans went from having kings and queens, to becoming a republic, to transforming to The Roman Empire, the empire began with Ceaser, Augustus. Ceaser, Augustus was the first roman emperor, he gained supreme power, all to himself and created a dynasty that set the foundation for western civilization. He was the nephew of Julius Ceaser and was also adopted by Julius Ceaser. After the assassination of Julius Ceaser, Ceaser, Augustus inherited his property, money, and soldiers. He built a strong army and joined forces with Mark Antony and Lepidus, they formed the Second Triumvirate. After forming the Second Triumvirate, he avenged the murder of Julius Ceaser in the Battle of

Philippi. The battle victory brought an end to

the 500-year-old republic and began the

Roman Empire. The Second Triumvirate

divided up the land, Ceaser, Augustus took

over the western land, Mark Antony took

over the eastern land, and Lepidus took over

north Africa. One day, Ceaser, Augustus

tried to give his sister Octavia, to Mark

Antony to be his wife, but Mark Antony

refused and turned down Octavia, because he was in love with the Queen of Africa, Egypt, Cleopatra. This made Ceaser, Augustus jealous and dislike Cleopatra, the Queen of Africa, Egypt. First Ceaser, Augustus kicked Lepidus out of the Second Triumvirate, then he convinced the senate to declare war on Cleopatra, the Queen of Africa, Egypt and Mark Antony, saying,

"Mark Antony has lost his roman ways", because he married the Queen of Africa, Egypt, Cleopatra. Ceaser, Augustus then goes to war with Cleopatra, the Queen of Africa, Egypt and Mark Antony in the naval Battle of Actium, and is victorious. After defeating Cleopatra, the Queen of Africa, Egypt and Mark Antony, Ceaser, Augustus gains all power, he controlled the western land, the eastern land, and north Africa. He made deals with the senate to bring together all the power and control for himself, and he disguised his power and control by keeping the government and political shapes the same, creating the Principate Period. This created the Golden Age for the roman civilization and the Roman Empire conquered modern-day Hungary, Croatia, Albania, Slovenia,

Austria, Serbia, Germany, Portugal, Switzerland, and Spain. The Roman agriculture, economy, and arts, began to thrive during this time. During this time Ceaser, Augustus did many things. Ceaser, Augustus-created the first, institutionalized police force, firefighting force, and praetorian guard force.

Ceaser, Augustus-increased the birth rate,

by making adultery illegal and creating

penalties for childless marriages.

Ceaser, Augustus-created tax reforms,

raising tax rates, increasing Rome's treasury.

Ceaser, Augustus-changed the name of the

8th month of the year, to August.

Ceaser, Augustus-built many fascinating

buildings.

Ceaser, Augustus-ruled for over 37 years, and even after his death the Roman Empire flourished for more than 200 years.

The first roman emperor to claim and announce Christianity was Constantine I. He developed his own version of Christianity, and made it a state religion, of the Roman Empire. He was the first to hold a church meeting, it became known as the Church Council of

Nicea, and it produced the Nicene creed. Constantine I, made the catholic church a business, and a powerful institution. Constantine I, help shape European civilization and established Christian teachings and understanding for future generations, he used Christianity as a weapon. Constantine I, renamed the Roman capitol Byzantine, to Constantinople and ruled there for over 30 years, longer than any other emperor since Ceaser, Augustus. He expanded the Roman Empire and built buildings like churches, and stadiums for chariot racing, a spectacle sport, like modern-day football, basketball, or baseball, which is roman tradition. Almost all of Rome would follow Constantine I, and his religion and go east to Constantinople. In 476, the Roman

Empire was conquered and then there was no emperor to challenge the pope, then the pope became powerful. The fall of the Roman Empire started a battle in western Europe between the popes and the kings for power.

THE RENAISSANCE

After the fall of the Roman Empire, Europeans experienced a long time of cultural decline. Centuries later, around the 12th century, Italian republics arose and formed the Italian Renaissance. The word renaissance means rebirth, revival, or renew. This is where modern-day European culture begins. The Renaissance was a time of personality, awakened consciousness in ancient culture, and invention, it was a time of devotion to ancient Rome and ancient Greece, as the origins of European civilization, and it reflected in their art and architecture. During this time of rebirth, the Italians learned how to value the goodness of a human being and how to apply that goodness to their lives, their philosophy was humanism. It all began in the 12th century, and the two strongest republics in Italy were Florence and Sienna. Sienna, Italy didn't have an ocean, river, or any body of water nearby, so they designed and built a network of underground, circular shaped tunnels, to transport water into the city. The underground tunnels had water flowing through them going into various parts of the city, wherever water was needed, and disposing into holding tanks and fountains. The most famous fountain in Sienna, Italy, was the Fonte Gaia. The Sienese used a stick, string, and stone to measure and make sure that the water flowed evenly into the Fonte Gaia. The water attracted many Italians and raised tensions in Florence, Italy. Sienna and Florence eventually fought for economic, political, and artistic power, the war was named the Battle of Montaperti. In the end, the Sienese came out on top with the victory and claimed dominant power in Italy. The Sienese began to do business international, construct churches, and schools, but then something unanticipated happened. In 1347, a disease broke out, killing around 70 percent of the Sienese population, the name of the disease was Black Death. There was a writer by the name of Giovanni Boccaccio who witnessed the Black Death, he described the disease saying, *"The Black Death killed so fast that you could lunch with your friends and then dine with your ancestors in heaven"*. After the Black Death, Sienna, Italy fell into decline, and never recovered. The Black Death also effected Florence, Italy, killing around 50 percent of the city's population, but Florence, Italy did recover. It took Florence, Italy more than a half a century to recover, but they recovered strong. The rich families of Tuscany, Italy put their money together and repaired the Italian cities. The rich business owners became the leaders and

Medici led the way, he went from running banks and businesses to running cities. Wealth brought power, and power brought art and architecture.

This is the time when that nameless writer, could become the great author, and that nameless builder, could become the great architect. Many buildings were constructed during the Italian Renaissance, the one building that stands out from the rest is a cathedral church, named the Santa Maria del Fiore. It was the largest church built at the time, and it is still one of the largest churches in the world now. The church was designed by Arnolfo di Cambio, it was designed to have a dome, but he died before it was completed. The church stood for decades without a roof top, until Filippo

Brunelleschi was assigned to work on it. Filippo Brunelleschi learned architecture by studying roman architecture in Rome, he was fascinated with the Pantheon dome, which spanned 142 feet. He designed one of the largest domes in the world for the Santa Maria del Fiore, by creating a dome within a dome. When standing inside the church, you can see the wonderful, decorated internal dome, and when standing outside the church you see the attractive, large external dome, which is essentially an outer shell protecting the inner dome. After around 16 years of construction, Filippo Brunelleschi completed the largest masonry dome in the world on August 30, 1436. Then after the completion of the Santa Maria del Fiore, Filippo Brunelleschi began to study in perspective and mathematical proportions. He created the Single Point Perspective, the idea that things appear to get smaller as they get further away, with everything coming all together towards a single vanishing point, on the horizon line. With this technique you can draw objects on a piece of paper and make them look three-dimensional and realistic, this is how the idea of a blue print came into existence. Before there were blue prints, there were actual models, the blue print changed architecture, allowing people to deduce the mathematics and put it on paper, to be exact. This new idea changed the world of art and architecture. The success of the Italian Renaissance restarted old rivalries, and artist who had turned into architects and engineers were drafted into war. Leonardo da Vinci and Michelangelo were best known for their works of art, but they also worked as military engineers during the Italian Renaissance. The Italian Renaissance created builders and artist, who created monuments and art, but the new age designed innovative technology for war.

MARTIN LUTHER

Martin Luther is one of the best role models, in the history of Christianity. He was a German monk, who fought for what was right against the most powerful forces of his time. Martin Luther set human beings free from mental imprisonment, mental slavery, and he was willing to die for what his conscience said was right. He was born in eastern Germany, in the Roman Empire, on November 10, 1483. During the middle ages the catholic church was the most powerful institution in Europe. Christianity was used systematically as a weapon during this time, the catholic church controlled everything. Christianity became a law, in the legal system, and was the only religion that could be practiced during this time.

Christianity was a form of tax and if you did not pay, you would be sent to court and forced to pay. The catholic church was in charge of if everyone's marriages were lawful, if everyone's birth was accepted, and if everyone's wills were valid. The catholic church made rules and laws to control the everyone's lives. Even the image of Christ was systematically altered everywhere, the people thought the catholic church was good and was blinded because of the churches promise of heaven. The church taught that money is the root of all evil, and if you followed its rules and participated in its rituals, you would be free from all evil, and have eternal happiness in heaven. This is how Europeans lived, for over a thousand years.

In 1505, the disease named the Black Death hit again, without warning, it had already killed about half of Europe's population in the previous 100 years. The Black Death touched Martin Luther personally, it killed 3 of his friends. The fear of gods power changed his life forever. Martin Luther made a vow to god and swore to become a monk. He stopped doing what his parents wanted him to do, he stopped doing what society said he should do, and he devoted himself to the spirit of god, he joined a monastery and became a monk. By becoming a monk, he cut himself off from the world and gave up on what the world considered as valuable, comfortable, and important, he believed that this was the only way to be truly saved. As a monk, Martin

Luther gathered with the other monks, 7 times out of the day to meditate, pray, and sing parts of the service, he developed into an honest and great monk. In 1510, he was sent to Rome, and took a 2-month pilgrimage. Rome was considered the holy city at the time, thousands of people would travel their every year to try and develop a better relationship with god. Martin Luther arrived in Rome just as the Renaissance was reaching its height, Michelangelo was painting the ceiling in the Sistine Chapel and Raphael was decorating the pope's apartment. Rome disappoints Martin Luther, and he quickly discovers that Rome is not a holy city. He realizes the pope has all the power and even controls the military. In the monastery, he realizes that businessmen, owners, and politicians rose to the top of the catholic church and the church is more of a business than a religion. Martin Luther got offended when he had to pay a fee for a piece of paper that granted him forgiveness for all his sins and punishment after death, this piece of paper was named an indulgence. Martin Luther disliked Rome, he felt that Rome was deceiving people and did not represent what Christianity really was about, he began to doubt everything and everyone around him. In 1511, Martin Luther left Rome and went to a smaller monastery in Wittenberg, Germany, the leader there was Johann Von Staupitz, he helped Martin Luther. He put Martin Luther in charge of bible studies at the University of Wittenberg. During this time Martin Luther studies, the bible in Latin, Greek, and Hebrew editions, he once said, *"If ever a monk had gotten to heaven by monkery, it was I"*. After studying the bible in 3 different editions he realizes that what he was taught by the catholic church was a lie. He was taught that you must go to church, and pay a fee to be saved, but he discovered that all you must do is have faith and give god your open heart, mind, and soul, to receive the gift that god has for you. He realizes that you don't need a priest, a church, or rituals, all you need is a direct one on one relationship with god. After discovering this Martin Luther says, *"I felt myself to have been born again, and it is as if I have entered through the open gates into heaven already"*.

After 7 years pass, Leo X, was the pope of Rome. Leo X, was a man devoted to the physical pleasures of the flesh. He threw parties with cakes, from which naked little boys would jump out from. After a few years of partying, he emptied the pope's treasury, and to refill the treasury, he turned to the catholic churches indulgences. He changed the indulgences, making them more expensive and attractive, and hired help to sale them.

The indulgences became the main market for sales in the Roman Empire, making a lot of money. The people thought that they needed this piece of paper, to be free from their sins and to enter heaven, that's how the indulgences made a lot of money.

Eventually, the new indulgences reached Martin Luther in Wittenberg, Germany, he was furious. Martin Luther noticed everyone around him spending their hard-earned money on the indulgences to be saved, and he knew it was a lie. He learned that to be saved was a gift from god, through faith, and on October 31, 1517, Martin Luther wrote a 95 power-point, statement letter aimed at the pope and the indulgences, the name of this letter became the 95 Theses. The 95 Theses, was 95 reasons why the pope, the church, and the indulgences were wrong. After writing the 95 Theses, he nailed it to the door of the Wittenberg Castle Church. The 95 Theses was a piece of paper challenging the power of the pope, it said statements like, *"Gods blessings are freely available for everyone, without the keys of the pope"*, and it also said statements like, *"Forgiveness of sins is in repentance, faith, and belief"*. Then someone made a copy of the 95 Theses and had it printed and sent all throughout Europe, the word spread out fast and created a revolution. Martin Luther said, *"Because you have corrupted gods truth, may god destroy you in this fire, I am not afraid of anyone and I rejoice to suffer in so noble of a cause".* When the word spread out about Martin Luther and got back to Rome, he was labeled a heretic. The punishment for being a heretic was death without blood, which meant that they set you on fire and burned you to death, or they would drown you to death. Martin Luther never backed down, after being labeled a heretic he continued to spread out his ideas and created an open letter to the Christian Nobility and directed it to the rulers of Germany. The open letter to the Christian Nobility began by saying, "*The grace and peace of god be with thee, the time to keep silent has passed, and the time to speak and come together has come*". Martin Luther printed this letter and sent it to all the leaders of Germany. Germany was a patchwork of tiny, different land, and each land had its own local ruler, all under the domination of the Roman Empire. He understood that only people in power could make a change, and individually the tiny, different lands could not stand up to Rome's financial demands, but all together they could. He once said, *"A real Christian life is hard, not easy"*. In 1521, pope Leo X, excommunicated Martin Luther from the catholic church, which meant that if he died without being reconciled with the church, he would spend eternity in hell. The roman emperor Charles V, got involved after the open letter to the Christian Nobility. Martin Luther also once said, *"I not only spread the word of the truth, I also defend it with my blood in death"*. The power of the 2 most powerful people, the emperor and the pope, meant nothing to Martin Luther, he continued to spread his ideas, he created a new system of faith, and named it The Babylonian Captivity of the Church. In the Babylonian Captivity of the Church, he says, *"Babylon is the city of evil, and the church has been kidnapped and taken to the evil city of Babylon, the church has been* taken over by evil men and put in prison, the church has got to be set free from imprisonment and let out of Babylon". The Babylonian Captivity of the Church also says, "there are only 2 holy sacraments and they are the Lords Super and Baptism, the Lords Super is everyone eating at one table, symbolizing equality for everyone, this is gods body of faith, and baptism *symbolizes the introduction of you to the people of god".* Martin Luther printed his new system of faith, sent it out, and it spread out throughout Europe quickly. Martin Luther also once said, *"I believed freely, and I was not a slave to the authority of no one".* His ideas spread all throughout Europe, creating a revolution, it is because of Martin Luther, Christianity is not controlling everyone, and there are different forms of Christianity. Martin Luther once said, "Even if the present age condemns me, maybe the judgements of future generations would be better", he also once said, "When I die, I want to be a ghost, so I can haunt the godless monks, the godless pope, and the godless emperor, until they have more trouble with a dead Martin Luther, than *they could have had before with a thousand living ones"*. This is the man Martin Luther King Jr. was named after.

ABRAHAM LINCOLN

Abraham Lincoln was the 16th president of the United States of America, he wrote the Emancipation Proclamation, that declared the freedom of slaves within the south Confederacy, in 1863. He was president during one of the bloodiest wars, the civil war. Abraham Lincoln was born on February 12, 1809, in Kentucky. He grew up on a farm and worked with his father until he was 21. During his childhood, he had less than one year of formal education, but he read as much as he could, he learned to educate himself. He once said, *"First I see what I read, then I hear what I read, 2 physical senses must catch the idea, that helps me understand it better"*, he was a self-taught man. Around 1831, he moved to

New Salem, a village with about 100 people and he would work there as a store clerk. In 1832, Indians invaded, led by Chief Black Hawk, and tried to reclaim their homelands by force. Then Abraham Lincoln enlisted to fight in the Black Hawk War and was chosen to be a captain. After the Black Hawk war, he ran for state legislator, at the age of 23, and lost. Although he lost, his actions say a lot about his character, it showed self-confidence, and ambition, as a young man. A few years later, he tried again to run for state legislator, and this time he was elected as a Whig to the Illinois legislator. After that, he taught himself law, passed the bar exam, and earned a lawyer's license. He then moved to the new state capitol and became a lawyer. Abraham

Lincoln became known as an honest lawyer and earned the nickname Honest Ab, he said, *"If you cannot be an honest lawyer, choose another profession, a worse man cannot be found, than one who stirs up strife to put money in his pocket".* In 1846, Abraham Lincoln enters politics on the national level, winning a congressional seat. In Washington D.C. he has his first deep encounter with slavery. Around this time slavery had already existed in America for about 200 years and was mainly in the south. Across the street from the White House, there were slave auction houses, these were houses where slaves were being treated and sold like animals, the United States Constitution allowed slavery.

In 1854, Abraham Lincoln was elected to the state legislator but resigned to run for United States senate, his opponent was Stephen Douglas. During this time, slavery was the political topic, and the territories of Kansas and Nebraska were no longer free areas, they were opened to slavery. The United States Constitution allowed the southern states to count their slaves as three-fifths of a person, for taxation and for determining representatives in congress. The northern states looked upon slavery as power for the southern states, because the south could use their slave power to dominate the federal government. So, the northerners formed a political party, and named it the Republicans, and made Abraham Lincoln the leader. Abraham

Lincoln once said, *"Slavery made a true democracy impossible"*, he saw the contradiction of the country saying it was a democratic society, but how, if it also owned slaves. Abraham Lincoln went head to head with Stephen Douglas for the state senate, it became known as the Lincoln-Douglas debates. The main topic was slavery, the democratic opponent Stephen Douglas said, "This government was made for the benefit of white men, the signers of the declaration of independence did not want negroes, savage Indians, or any barbaric race to benefit, and any state or territory that wants slavery should be allowed to have it". Abraham Lincoln said, "I am against slavery, but slaves should be sent back to Africa and colonized, blacks and whites *should live separated"*. Stephen Douglas won the state election, and that says a lot about how things were. Although Abraham Lincoln lost the state election to Stephen Douglas, it gave him popularity and a national reputation, that later got him nominated for the presidency by the republican party. Abraham Lincoln won the presidential election in 1860, without the support of southern states. The south was furious, the south did not want the northern republican party to take over the federal government or take away their slaves, because that was their form of power, the south had over 4 million slaves, the slaves are what made the south a powerful force. So, then the southern states got together and formed the Confederate States of

America. Out of 34 United States, 7 slave states formed the Confederate States of America, and 4 other states were considered border neutral states, the neutral states also owned slaves. The south armed themselves and fired the first shot, and in 1861, the civil war began. The president of the southern Confederate states was Jefferson Davis, and their army leader was Robert E. Lee, and the army leader of the Union sates was Ulysses S. Grant. The southern Confederate army dominated the war with the help of slaves, until 1863. In 1863, Abraham Lincoln wrote the Emancipation Proclamation, redirecting the civil war and taking away the power of the south. The Emancipation Proclamation stated, *"all individuals held as slaves in rebellious states, are set free"*. Then Abraham Lincoln turned to Africans for help in the war, he said, *"You will not fight to free negroes, but some of them are willing to fight for you, in peace, there will be a black man who can remember with a silent tongue and a well-aimed gun, blacks help mankind to this great consummation"*, then he recommended black votes. Over 170,000

Africans joined the Union army and help defeat the south. Abraham Lincoln argued with congress to pass a 13th Amendment to the constitution, to end slavery and it passed after his death. Abraham Lincoln also once said, *"The war might be gods punishment on all Americans for 200 years of slavery"*.

THE GREAT DEPRESSION

The Great Depression was an economic downfall that lasted 10 years. Production, distribution, and income was at an all-time low in the United States of America, from 1929 to 1939, the economic downfall effected the entire world. On October 24, 1929, stock traders sold 12.9 million shares of stock in one day, more than doubling the usual amount, the name of that day is Black Thursday. Over the next few days, stock prices fell over 21 percent, creating the Stock Market Crash of 1929, it wiped out millions of investors. The stock market crash, along with years of agricultural decline in the southeastern region of the United States, where farmers grew the main crops, caused the Great Depression.

During this time Herbert Hoover was the 31st president of the United States of America. His first thought about the situation was that it was just a little recession, no worse than the recession the nation faced after World War I. But he was wrong, the depression steadily worsened, pushing millions into poverty. Large employers shut down their businesses, people lost their jobs, and farmers lost their farms. Many people were getting evicted from their homes, becoming homeless, and hopeless, not knowing where their next meal was coming from, many people starved to death. It was worse for Africans, during these tough times the number of lynching's doubled. Some Americans took their hardships, frustrations, and anger out on Africans, for example, here is a poem, that was turned into a song, sung by Billie Holiday, called Strange Fruit, it describes the lynching's in the south during the Great Depression.

"Southern trees bear strange fruit, Blood on the leaves and blood at the root;

Black bodies swinging in the southern breeze,

Strange fruit hanging from the poplar trees;

The African Philosophy

Pastoral scene of the gallant south, The

bulging eyes and the twisted mouth;

Scent of magnolias sweet and fresh, Then

the sudden smell of burning flesh;

Here is fruit for the crows to pluck, For the

rain to gather for the wind to suck;

For the sun to rot for the trees to drop, Here

is a strange and bitter crop;"

During the Great Depression, president Herbert Hoover signed a law that made the star-spangled banner, Americas national anthem. The star-spangled banner is based on an 1814 poem, by Francis Scott Key, here is a verse from the poem.

"Their blood has washed out, their foul footsteps pollution;

No refuge could save the hireling and slave

from the terror of flight or the gloom of the

grave;

And the star-spangled banner in triumph doth

wave;

Over the land of the free and home of the

brave;"

By 1931, over 800 banks throughout the

country had failed, and the people had fallen

into despair. President Herbert Hoover said, *"the government should not help the people during challenging times"*, he refused to use the power of the federal government. He refused to use federal money to provide direct help for the poor people in need, banks, or public projects. He said, *"it was not the government's responsibility to create jobs or provide relief"*, he believed that for people to get help, some people should volunteer to help at the local level to raise money.

Any group of people who have been subjected to unemployment, can't feed their families, and must watch their family suffer over an extended period, will rebel against their oppressors, and this is what happens. In Arkansas, farmers marched to a grocery store, demanding food, because they were starving to death. In the Detroit area, the people marched to the Ford Motor Company, where over 37,000 people had lost their job, the people demanded relief money for being laid off, and clashed head to head with the police, 4 protesters were killed that day. Then the military veterans got together from all over the country and marched to the white house in Washington D.C. The veterans demanded a check for their services in World War I, the check became known as the Bonus Check, and the veterans became known as the Bonus Army. Thousands of veterans poured into Washington D.C. and stayed there, demanding a Bonus Check. The veterans formed an army over 21,000 people and created their own community there, it was named the Bonus Army Camp.

President Herbert Hoover got the military involved, instead of helping the veterans, creating a war, he had hundreds of soldiers accompanied by tanks, evict the veterans out of Washington D.C.

By the presidential election in 1932, Herbert Hoover was disliked and unpopular, he was easily defeated by Franklin D. Roosevelt. As soon as Franklin D. Roosevelt became the

32nd president of the United States of America, he funded different federal programs for restoring the United States American economy, helping the unemployed and he also reformed the system, so a stock market crash wouldn't happen again. The economy improved throughout the next 7 years.

MARTIN LUTHER KING JR.

Martin Luther King Jr. is one of the greatest leaders and one of the greatest role models, of all time. He fought for justice, righteousness, freedom, peace, and equality, for all human beings. Martin Luther King Jr. was born on January 15, 1929, the

The African Philosophy

year the Great Depression began. During this time, Africans were free from being slaves but were still treated very unfairly because of how the laws were. Africans were denied basic human rights, Africans were not allowed to vote, Africans could not use public facilities or transportation on an equal basis with whites, and Africans had to attend inferior separate schools, away from whites. Martin Luther King Jr. grew up in the south, in Atlanta, Georgia, where it was hard for Africans. He learned to value education and excelled in school. By the time he was 18, he was an ordained minister, and at 19, he graduated from Morehouse College, then entered Crozer Theological Seminary, in Pennsylvania, he studied religion and philosophy.

Martin Luther King Jr. studied men like Henry David Thoreau, an American writer and philosopher, who lived during the 19th century. Henry David Thoreau believed that people should not obey unjust laws, and you should be willing to accept the punishment from breaking the law, to influence others to want to change the law. He used a form of protest called passive resistance, which meant that his actions to get the law changed were done in a nonviolent way. In his situation, he refused to pay a church tax that was imposed by the local government. He did this because the United States Constitution provides for the separation of the church and the state, he felt that the tax was unjust and didn't pay for it, he was sent to jail but went willingly, and it got the attention of others. Martin Luther King Jr. also studied men like Mahatma Gandhi, although he was a racist, who thought Africans were inferior, Martin Luther King Jr. respected his use of nonviolent resistance to free his people and gain his people their independence from Great Britain. Mahatma Gandhi and his movement went to jail many times for their nonviolent resistance, and after many years of resistance, protest, and jailing's, they won their independence for India in 1947. This is what Martin Luther King Jr. believed in, he said, *"The nonviolent movement is strong not weak, we are not engaged in this battle where we sit down and do nothing, there is a big difference between nonresistance to evil, and nonviolent resistance to evil.*

Nonresistance leaves you in a state of complacency, and nonviolent resistance means you do resist, in a strong, righteous, and determined way". He also said, "Killing is a tragic way to deal with any social problem, violence only leads to new and more social complex problems. There is no violent solution to the problem that the African confronts in this world, the people *who are starving to death, getting shot, and going to jail, are African, this is a moral problem that must be fixed"*.

After Martin Luther King Jr. graduated from Crozer Theological Seminary and got his master's degree, he went to Boston University to get his doctorate in philosophy. In 1954, he became a pastor at Dexter Baptist Church in Montgomery,

The African Philosophy

Alabama, this is where he began to shine like the sun. During this time, if a white person wanted to ride the bus, they would just get on the bus, pay a fare, and then take a seat. But if an African wanted to ride the bus, they would get on the bus, pay a fare, then get off the bus, and walk to the back door of the bus, and then get back on that way. Africans could only sit on the back of the bus, and if the seats were filled, an African had to give up their seat to any white person that got on the bus. In Alabama, December of 1955, Rosa Parks made an action that got the attention of Martin Luther King Jr. and created a movement. Rosa Parks was a black woman who took a seat on a bus, on her way home from work. The bus seats got filled up with passengers and then a white man got on the bus, the bus driver told Rosa Parks to give her seat up to the white man, she refused. The bus driver called the police on her, and she was taken to jail. This incident caused the African community to boycott the bus line, and no African person rode the bus until Africans were given equal treatment. The African community formed a group called the Montgomery, Alabama

Improvement Association, and picked Martin Luther King Jr. to be the leader. Martin Luther King Jr. once said, *"When a pharaoh wanted to prolong a period of slavery, he had a secret formula for doing it, he would keep the slaves fighting each other, but when the slaves got together, they got out of slavery"*. African ministers were encouraged by the movement and formed the Southern Christian Leadership Conference and elected Martin Luther King Jr. to be the president. Eventually all public facilities became available to all people on an equal basis, and because of racism, this made some white people hate Martin Luther King Jr. Even the leader of the FBI, J. Edgar Hoover, hated Martin Luther King Jr. and labeled him as one of the most dangerous people in the United States of America. Martin Luther King Jr. received death threats, his house was bombed, and he went to jail many times for disobeying unjust laws, but he never changed, he continued to preach nonviolence, peace, equality, justice, and love. Martin Luther King Jr. said, *"Love is strong not weak, love is not an emotional mixture, love is the desire for something, love is a strong force, and when you organize love it becomes a powerful force*". This inspired the civil-rights movement, and the movement destroyed the structure of segregation.

The civil-rights movement was a human-rights movement, that had its own version of criminality, they didn't mind getting arrested if the law was unjust. The civil-rights movement led nonviolent protest against unequal treatment in voting, employment, education, housing, health-care, restaurants, and much more, against nearly all unequal aspects of life. Martin Luther King Jr. once said, *"For years now I have heard the word wait, it rings in the ear of every negro with piercing familiarity, this wait has almost always meant never, justice to long delayed, is justice denied"*. In 1963, Martin Luther King Jr. led a march on Washington D.C. and more than 200,000 people attended. In his I Have a Dream speech, he spoke for every human being in the world who believed in justice, freedom, and equality. In 1964, he was awarded the Nobel Peace Prize for his work. Martin Luther King Jr. said, *"A Nobel Prize is not important to me, what is important to me is how I gave my life serving others, how I tried to love, how I fed the homeless and the hungry, how I clothed those who were naked, how I helped those who were imprisoned, and how I was right about the war question, this is what was important to me".* He also once said, *"In my nonviolent movement I could see the reaction of the white community, it aroused a sense of shame within them all, righteousness touches the conscience and establishes a sense of guilt and repentance, it disturbs their sense of contentment, white people in power are not comfortable about a nonviolent movement".*

MODERN DAY SLAVERY

After the assassination of great African leaders like Martin Luther King Jr., Malcom X, and Fred Hampton, African communities were defenseless, weak, and vulnerable, then the Africans were instantly attacked.

Africans are a planned minority, after slavery,

Africans were labeled as 2nd class citizens, which means modern-day slave. The attack on Africans was strategic, in the past Africans were controlled by force, now Africans are controlled psychologically. First, the perception of the African was criminalized. The images and specific language that was used to criminalize the African was so deceiving, Africans were afraid of themselves, then a political force came and demolished the African communities. The political force attack on Africans began in 1970, with terms like law and order and the war on drugs, these terms were directed towards Africans, law and order meant, locking Africans in jail, and the war on drugs meant, a war on Africans. These terms were introduced by Richard Nixon the 37th president of the United States of

America, this modern attack on Africans has lasted over 47 years, there is still a war on Africans now. This war on drugs criminalized all Africans and systematically destroyed African lives, African families, and African communities. The worse attack on Africans, that did the most damage, came in 1993, when Bill Clinton became the 42nd president of the United States of America, he set the foundation for modern day slavery. Around 100 years ago, some white people would put on white sheets and use blood hound dogs against the African, now they have taken off the white sheets and put on police uniforms and traded in the blood hound dogs for K-9 dogs. Bill Clinton spent billions of dollars to build prisons, to militarize law enforcement, and to enforce new laws that made the system how it is today. Africans were criminalized even more, thrown in jail even more, and laws increased the amount of time Africans spent in jail even more. After Bill Clinton, the African abuse continued with George W. Bush. George W. Bush was the 43rd president of the United States and he continued to criminalize the African and lock them in cages like animals. His grandfather,

Prescott Bush, was a politician who supported and help finance Hitler, who was a white supremacist. George W. Bush made a lot of bad decisions as president, his worst decision was to begin a war in 2003, against Iraq, which lasted 7 around years. After the planes crashed on September 11, 2001, George W. Bush said, *"Our god is the god who named the stars"*, meaning white supremacy. The American people disliked him so much, the first black president was elected in 2009, Barack Hussein Obama II. Barack Hussein Obama II, was the 44th president of the United States of America and was one of the greatest presidents of all time, but some white people hated him because of racism, racism is something that Africans still face today. Barack Hussein

Obama II, once said, *"Change will not come if we wait for some other person or some other time, we are the ones we have been waiting for, we are the change that we seek"*. His father was a governmental economist, from Africa, Kenya, after everything Africans have been through, one of us has achieved the greatest achievement possible, by becoming the president of the United States of America.

Africans are great, the African can achieve anything, this is why Africans are killed, jailed, exiled, and held down, because white people in power, fear black power. Barack Hussein Obama II, did many remarkable things for Africans, he helped African business, African young males, African farmers and he reduced incarceration for the first time in 40 years, he also was the first president to visit a prison. Barack Hussein Obama II, did a lot for Africans but there is only so much he could do in an evil, hateful, ungodly, and unspiritual system. The system is corrupt, how was it possible for Barrack Hussein Obama II, to become president? In 1964, a civil-rights activist by the name of Jimmie Lee Jackson was killed by a state trooper in Alabama, then the civil-rights movement organized a march over his death, the march brought into being the voting rights bill, which came in 1965, if it was not for Jimmie Lee Jacksons death, Barack Hussein Obama II, would have never became president. Sometimes you must die for the greater cause, we all have a part to play in the Universe. Barack Hussein Obama II, also once said, *"If you're walking down the right path and you're willing to keep walking, you'll make progress"*. After having the first black president elected, the racist in the world got organized and elected Donald Trump, he is currently the 45th president of the United States of America. There is a large segment of America that believes Africans have no place in America, intellectually or politically. To get elected, Donald Trump said things like, *"In the good* old days this doesn't happen because they use to treat them very rough, and when they protested once, they would not do it again so easily", and Donald Trump also said, "I love the old days, you know what they use to do to guys like that in a place like this? They would be carried out on a stretcher folks". Donald Trump also bluntly said, "I am the law and order candidate".

Different systems of oppression have led the African to where Africans are today. Out of 44 different presidents, 42 of them are descendants of the King of England, John Lackland, the 2 that are not descendants are Martin Van Buren and Donald Trump, this is not a coincidence. The Americas have always been owned and ruled by a secret society, members of British and French royal bloodlines, the royal families of Britain and Europe, who stole wealth, power, and the Holy Grail, from the Knights Templar. The presidents of the United States of America, were part of a royal dynasty. For white power, Africans have been through colonialism, genocide, and have been brutalized for over 400 years, and it continues. Africans use to get raped, burned, cut, ripped apart, and hung, now there are over 2 million human beings locked up behind bars, human beings are not born to be locked up in a cage, 1 out of 3 African males are expected to go to prison. All throughout history, Africans have been controlled by this secret society's systematic white power. Africans are controlled by means of money, beliefs, and attitudes, and inequality, injustice, division, and racism, are empowering white supremacy.

It was slavery and cheap labor before, now it's

mass incarceration and the prison Industrial

system.

THE UNIVERSAL SPIRIT

There is a universal energy in the Universe, that is within all of nature. All human beings have some of the same qualities. All human beings have the desire for attention, power, importance, and first place leadership. This is the Universal spirit that is within all human beings. It begins when we are first brought into this world, as a baby you cry for attention naturally, and life puts you in first place. This cry for attention never leaves, it stays with you throughout your adulthood, for example, when you do something good you want to be praised for it. This praise, attention, and feelings of importance, feeds your ego, and for some people it makes them unhappy when that praise, attention, and importance, is going to much towards somebody else. This praise, attention, and feelings of importance, makes people joiners, some people will join anything for recognition, attention, and praise. Certain names and logos are put on businesses, cars, and clothes, to become major, and this quest for recognition, praise, and attention, easily deceives you into valuing these certain names and logos. Human beings want to be praised, recognized, have attention, be the best, and out do others, that's why you want to drive that certain car and look that certain way, to make others watchful and envious of you. This spirit of wanting to be important, wanting to be praised, wanting to outdo others, wanting to be in first place, and have attention, takes over your life and never stops, it can become dangerous and destructive, that's why you must learn how to balance and control your spirit. If you don't learn how to balance and control your spirit, every day you will have to deal with your ego problem, by boasting, and this boasting causes the spirit to lie. Criminology tells us that human beings are driven to crime because of this spirit of wanting to be important, wanting to be praised, wanting to outdo others, wanting to be in first place, and have attention. These people are not getting enough recognition, praise, and attention, and are not treated fairly from their normal social behavior, so they turn to irrational social behavior to get the recognition, praise, and attention that they desire. So, they pick up a gun and go rob a store for that spirit of importance, recognition, praise, and attention. This confused spirit that we develop makes you push others down, to lift yourself up, and this leads to degrading actions like gossip, people will spread out the most false, evil things about a person to lift themselves up.

Your main goal in life should be to balance and control this spirit, and if you don't this spirit grows into snobbish and social exclusiveness. For example, these people would say, *"I'm in this fraternity and its better than yours, and no one else can get into this fraternity"*. These things become so exclusive, people act as if every human being is not equal, another example is, when people get their bachelor's degree, master's degree, or doctoral degree, they act as if they are a better human being than others. Just because you have some training, that does not make you a better human being than others, it just means that you are trained, but this confused spirit of snobbish, social exclusiveness will have you thinking incorrectly. This applies to anything, for example, just because you have more economic security, that does not make you a better human being than a person who doesn't have that economic security, all human beings are equal.

This unbalanced and uncontrolled spirit of wanting to be important, wanting to be praised, wanting to outdo others, wanting to be in first place, and have attention, also leads to evil qualities, such as unfairness, selfishness, and racism. For example, white people thought that segregation was right, and intermarriage was wrong. Now the average white person, lives like the average black person and we all should be fighting for equal rights. White people are put in the position of supporting the oppressor because of racism and being blind, they don't see that the same evil forces that oppress Africans all around the world, are the same evil forces oppressing average white people. The only thing average white people are living on is the satisfaction of their skin being white, the spirit of thinking they are somebody because of their white skin, but they are so poor they can't even pay for their kids to go to college. The only thing the average white person has going for themselves is a false feeling that they are superior because of their skin. All human beings need to join forces and fight for what is right, which is equality, justice, and freedom, all human beings are equal. What is wrong in the world today is all the nations of the world are engaged in a big contest for supremacy. If a revolution doesn't happen now and stop this trend, human beings won't be here much longer for anything. The corrupting nature of power is universal. All good human beings must unite and bring an end to this evil force that we see in the world today, if we don't someone will make that mistake of dropping a nuclear bomb, starting a nuclear war. They have bombs right now in China that could destroy

Washington D.C. within 3 seconds, everyone would be wiped away. This is the direction we are headed in because of this spirit, every nation wants to be first, every nation wants to be ahead of everyone else and the leader, and the nation we are in now is the main culprit. The United States of America has engaged in pointless, senseless, and unjust wars, already, for example, the war in Iraq. The United States of America has committed more war crimes than any other nation in the world, and it never stops, this spirit becomes the pride, arrogance, and egotism of a nation. There is nothing wrong with wanting to be important, wanting to be praised, wanting to outdo others, wanting to be in first place or wanting to have attention, but you must balance and control your spirit. In this revolution the patterns of thought must change, there is a universal moral law within all human beings, the aim of life must be to contribute to the general good of the world, this is the purpose of a human being. Don't act justly in the fear of being caught, act justly because it is right. Acting justly is the way human existence must turn, human beings must go beyond their selfish biological needs, peel away the layers of ignorance, and love what is right and the behaviors of more than anything. You become a vehicle of the Universe by doing what is right, doing what is right has its own reward, it balances and controls desire, the spirit, and thinking. Desire to be the first to love, want to get praised for generosity, get attention from moral excellence, seek the best outcome for everyone without self-calculation, this is the absolute, true greatness of a human being. Life is meaningless if it lacks good actions, doing what is right naturally puts your mind at rest. If everyone acted like you, would it benefit the world? Your actions are to be judged by if they are universal, actions are to be judged according to whether you would be pleased if everyone in the world took the same actions, act according to which that it should become an Universal law. The universal moral law is timeless, space less, changeless, and perfect. The universal moral law is as real as the sun, the stars, the moon, and all the planets, and going against the universal moral law will make you frustrated, troubled, and unhappy. Happiness is not a pleasure, but a by-product of a good, disciplined life. Happiness comes from expressing what is good for the entire world, over the long term. The one who serves and helps the most people is the greatest. Absolute, true greatness comes not by favoritism, but by practice, condition, and fitness. Happiness and joy comes from moving away from the self by throwing yourselves into your passions and helping others. The purpose of a society, politics, media, and education is to promote was is good and right and the behaviors of, to make everyone better. Seek the good first, then everything else good will follow naturally, this is the natural, universal form of greatness. Everyone can be great this way, anyone can pursue their passions, and serve others, you don't need certain training, a college degree, or intelligence to help others, all you need is a heart full of grace, and a soul generated by love, then you can be the greatest and feel important, be praised, and desire the absolute, right, and universal kind of attention. The Universal spirit is what is right throughout the entire world, when you do what is right, you become part of the timeless, eternal, and universal spiritual expression of the Universe, and by doing what is right we create a world of equality, order, and peace.

THE REVOLUTION

The world is doomed, and all messed up.

The good people in the world have been

forced to a point to deal with the problems

man has been trying to deal with all

throughout history. Survival demands that

every good person engages in the struggle

and deal with the problems of the world.

The problems are injustice, the refusal to

be fair, and the refusal of honest equality.

People can no longer just talk about it, there must be a revolution, or their will be nonexistence. The African consciousness has awakened, the African is serious now and every African in the world must be determined to gain their rightful place in the Universe. The long years of poverty, neglect, and hurt are over, Africans are done living the way that they have been forced to live, say it proudly, *"I am a revolutionary"*. Africa has the most profitable natural resources, why are there over 12,000,000 Africans starving, with big heads, their ribs showing, and clouded eyes, all from malnutrition. Africans are starving to death in Africa, the number of Africans starving in Africa, is larger than the entire population in Belgium, Europe. There are over 2,000,000 African children under the age of five that are starving in Africa, becoming vulnerable to diseases such as the measles, malaria, and cholera. Africans are starving to death every few minutes in Africa, the world knows this information, and no one is helping. The good people in the world must deal with these problems of the poor and must be concerned about their brothers and sisters who can't eat 3 square meals a day and are starving to death. When human beings come together to do what is right and are willing to sacrifice for it, there is no such thing as losing, nothing can stop the spirit and the force of God, say it proudly, *"I am a revolutionary"*. The good people in the world must go about this the right way, don't get engaged in anything negative, no negative arguments, no negative protest, and no violence, that's not the right way. The good people in the world must be determined to do things right, be evolved, and mature men and women, in unity, this force is unstoppable.

America was built on a revolution, the American Revolutionary War was between groups of American colonist and British soldiers. Americans were fighting for their human rights, as subjects under the British power and domination. The movement for American independence from Britain grew large, then a 5-man committee including Thomas Jefferson, John Adams, and

Benjamin Franklin, wrote a formal statement of the American colonies intentions, they turned to the Magna Carta for encouragement. The Magna Carta was the first written constitution in European history, the 63 clauses symbolize freedom from oppression. Then on July 4, 1776, the congress formally accepted and embraced the Declaration of

Independence, which is the birth of American independence. The most famous part of the Declaration of Independence states, "We hold these truths to be self-evident; that all men are created equal; that they are endowed by their creator with certain inalienable rights; that among these are life, liberty, and the pursuit of happiness; that to secure these *rights, governments are instituted among men, deriving their just powers from the consent of the governed".* Then 11 years later the Constitution was created, it established Americas national government, fundamental laws, and it guarantees basic rights for its citizens. Along with the Constitution, came the Bill of Rights, which are 10 Amendments guaranteeing basic rights and protection for its citizens, such as the freedom to assemble and the freedom of speech. The Magna Carta is evident in the Declaration of Independence, the Constitution, and the Bill of Rights. The First Amendment of the Bill of Rights guarantees freedom of expression by stopping congress from restricting the rights of individuals to speak freely, the government cannot interfere. A person cannot be held liable, criminally or civilly for anything spoken or written about a person, organization, or topic. The First Amendment also guarantees the right of citizens to come together and gather peaceably and to petition their government. The people have the right to come together and ask the government to provide relief for a wrong through the courts or any other government action. The First Amendment guarantees the people freedom of assembly, freedom of speech, and the freedom of press, America must be true to what it said on paper, the greatness of America is the right to protest for a right.

The good people in the world must unite and fight for equality, justice, and righteousness. God is commanding the good people in the world to be concerned about the poor, the ghettos, the slums, and the people who can't eat 3 square meals a day and are starving to death. All the good people around the world must rise up and direct their action to the power of economic withdrawal. Individually Africans are poor, when you compare them to white society in America, but collectively, all Africans together are rich, Africans are richer than most nations in the world, collectively. The Africans annual income a year, number in the trillions, that's more than all the exports of the United States, and more than the national budget of

Canada. Africans have power, this is how you use it correctly. The good people in the world don't have to go around cursing, arguing, or acting bad. The good people in the world don't need bricks, Molotov cocktail bottles, or guns. The only thing the good people in the world have to do is go around to these big corporations and say, "God sent us here to say you're not *treating his children right, and we came by to ask you to make the first plan on your agenda fair treatment where Gods children are involved and concerned, and if your not prepared to do that we have an agenda that we must follow, which is withdrawing economic support from you"*. The good people in the world must stop spending their money with these major corporations such as Betty Crocker, Pillsbury, Axe body spray, Coca-Cola, Mazola Corn Oil, Kellogg's, and Nestle. Africans have been feeling all the pain and suffering, and now its time to redistribute the pain, say it proudly, *"I am a revolutionary"*. Start with these major companies because they aren't fair with their hiring policies, and the process must begin at the top, to do the most damage, which then trickles down. The good people in the world must force people to do what is right and force them to support the needs and human rights of Africans all around the world. All the good people around the world must unite and go on strike, take your money out of your bank account and deposit it in a good, proud African bank, the good people must create these institutions. Take your money out of your loaning association and deposit it in a good, proud African loaning association, the good people must create these institutions. Take your money out of your insurance company and deposit it in a good, proud African insurance company, the good people must create these institutions. Say it proudly, *"I am a revolutionary"*. All the good people, the rich, and the famous, must create these institutions and take the lead, then everyone else will follow. This is how you have a bloodless revolution, in the beginning process, Africans must build an economic base, and at the same time this will put pressure where it really hurts. All

The African Philosophy

the good people around the world must give themselves to this revolution until the end, everyone must believe in it, and see it through. Either all the good people in the world fight and go up together in this revolution or go down together and become extinct. All the good people around the world must learn to develop a kind of dangerous unselfishness for each other, and this will make the revolution an unstoppable force. When good people began fighting for what is right, other good people will join and make the force even more powerful. You must have determination in these powerful days of the revolution, all the good people must unite and make the world great, once and for all, creating a real democracy. Democracy is a

Greek word, meaning power of the people, in a democracy the people have the power, its time for all the good people around the world to come together and show the power of a real democracy. The good people in the world never cleaned up the filth from 400 years ago, the entire system must change, and now is the time to clean it up, say it proudly, *"I am a revolutionary"*.

The African Philosophy

Be in love with the commitment to this revolution, refuse to do anything that's not in the interest of the revolution. Freedom, equality, and justice is never voluntarily given by the oppressor, it must be demanded by the oppressed. Only all the good people together can eliminate the political, economic, and social injustice that confront Africans all around the world.

The African Philosophy

With a determined and powerful commitment, I believe that all the good people in the world can transform the dark yesterdays of injustice, into bright tomorrows of justice and humanity, everyone has a part to play, and a position to assume. Say it proudly 3 times, *"I am a revolutionary, I am a revolutionary, I am a revolutionary"*.

THE UNIVERSAL SPIRITUAL FATHER

All throughout history there has been different religions and different buildings constructed, all dedicated to honor, worship, and praise the universal Spiritual Father God, the Universe. The universal Spiritual Father God, the Universe, is real, there is a higher power, it gives life to, and it spiritually awakens a human being. Dedicate your life to, put total trust in, and honor the universal Spiritual Father God, the Universe, for this is the highest expression of a human being. A person that walks down this path may appear crazy, insane, or delirious, and may even seem unreasonable to the rest of humanity, but only because they are not relying on the wisdom of the universal Spiritual Father God, the Universe. If the universal Spiritual Father God, the Universe, moves in mysterious ways, then someone who is a vehicle for the universal Spiritual Father God, the Universe, will also move in mysterious ways. He who loved himself, became great through himself; he who loved others, became great through others; but he who loved the universal Spiritual Father God, the Universe, through his devotion, became greater than all. Faith is beyond what you see, words, and concepts, it is the highest passion in a human being. Elijah was an outlaw when the universal Spiritual Father God, the Universe, appeared to him in a vision. Paul wrote half of his works from a jail cell, his writings were inspired by the universal Spiritual Father God, the Universe, in which we still draw wisdom from today. Moses was a criminal, exiled from Egypt, Africa's penal system, he found his purpose by himself, and became a leader for the people. The Hebrews were slaves for over 400 years, then the universal Spiritual Father God, the Universe, transformed their suffering into power. Their oppressors became contributors, handing over the treasures of Egypt, Africa. What they intend to harm you with, deceive you with, and defeat you with, the universal Spiritual Father God, the Universe, will use to build you up with. The universal Spiritual Father, the Universe, puts you through training first. David had the courage, strength, and confidence, to square up against the most terrifying person imaginable, because he overcame different obstacles along the way, he thought of it as Gods training, for facing and defeating goliath. Don't let pain defeat you, use it as fuel for energy towards your passion, everyone has circumstances to overcome, to transcend them. There is only one universal Spiritual Father God, the

The African Philosophy

Universe, and our relationship with the Universe is sacred, private, and one on one. Only the Universe can save you, protect you from harm, give you enlightenment, and eternal peace. You are part of the Universe, the Universe is your Father, the same elements that are in the sun, the stars, the moon, and all the planets, are in you. Every individual is a piece of the universal

Spiritual Father God, the Universe, so treating another human being badly is like doing the same thing to yourself. Treat others how you want to be treated, there is no I, make your actions a universal expression of the righteous, timeless, and changeless spirit of the Universe. Africans have been learning from the enemy, a jealous, envious, hating, and evil adversary,

The African Philosophy

who does not want you to have your righteous place in the Universe. Look at history, Africans have been through the most in this Universe, but their spirit is still alive, Africans are immortal, Africans are the strongest, most righteous, and most spiritual beings in the Universe. Africans are the original beings of the earth, the gods of the earth, sent forth to illuminate, and shine bright like the sun star, brighten every place you go with truth, justice, righteousness, fearlessness, boldness, wisdom, and knowledge.

Life is about finding your purpose, listen to your conscience, there is a universal Spiritual Father, when the Universe speaks to you listen, don't doubt it, the Universe speaks in many different forms. You don't decide the next thought you think, the universal Spiritual Father God, the Universe does. Listen to nothing except your own voice and experiences. Seek to understand the Universe through spiritual practice, the absolute truth is beyond what you see, there is wholeness to the Universe, only human beings break things into parts and categories. Many human beings are called by the Universe, but few are chosen by the Universe. The Universe chooses the most faithful, righteous, and pure human beings, and if the Universe chooses you, you will know. You will have the magical eyes, ears, and mind of the Universe. You will see differently, hear differently, and think differently, from others. You will be able to see things as they are, and you will understand everything. When you are chosen you can't force other human beings to see and understand the way you do, you must teach. Teach in metaphors and in your actions. Have no fear, the Universe is in control, the Universe is with you always, and the Universe protects you. Live authentically, choose your own future instead of living blindly, accepting society's rules and moral laws of the day. Take control of the talents and possibilities that you do have and make something great out of it. Real glory is when you find your identity through your passions and express it through your words, deeds, and art. It is through the understanding of the power, of your gift, for you to escape the prison of despair. If you can help someone traveling in the wrong direction, then your living will not be in vain. Represent the Spiritual Father and all human beings, for we are all one. Each birth carries with it the possibility of a changed world, and with human beings as great as Africans, righteousness, peace, justice, and equality is possible, worldwide.

SUPERSTAR

If you can't be the lion than runs the jungle, be a deer near the

humble;

But be the best deer, and never tumble;

Be on the side of the real, and thank the Universe each time you

are still;

Make sure you are lovable, for everyone to see;

And plant each seed with meaning, so the fruit reveals the

purpose of the tree;

If you can't be the sun, be a star;

For its not about the size of the one, its about being the best of

who you are;

-MELVIN ORANGE JR.

The African Philosophy

The World is Turning in a False Direction, Enthroning False Gods. This Philosophy is an Accurate Account of the Universal Spiritual Father God, the Universe, He or She Who Believes In Me Will Live. Knowledge of the Universal Spiritual Father God, the Universe, is Empowering, and Spiritual Truths are Timeless, Changeless, and Perfect.

"Give a Man Food and You Feed Him for a Day, Teach a Man to Hunt and You Feed Him for Life".

-MELVIN ORANGE JR.

www.ingramcontent.com/pod-product-compliance
Lightning Source LLC
Chambersburg PA
CBHW060418010526
44118CB00017B/2270